First Edition 2013

1

Table of Contents

CHOCOLATE BROWNIES

NO-BAKE APPLE PIES
P{21}

P{22}

AMAZING BUTTER COOKIES

P{23}

MICROWAVE BANANA BREAD

P{24}

CHOCOLATE COCONUT FUDGE CUPS

P{25}

MINI PUMPKIN PIE

P{26}

PINEAPPLE MANGO BANANA SORBET

P{27}

COCONUT BUTTER DATES

Recipes Continued...

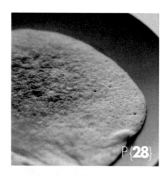

TWO-INGREDIENT PANCAKE
P{28}

COCONUT BANANA BALLS
P{29}

SUGAR-FREE GINGER SPICE COOKIES
P{30}

VANILLA MADELEINE COOKIES
P{31}

RAW COCONUT COOKIES
P{32}

SUGAR-FREE CHOCOLATE BISCOTTI
P{33}

COFFEE CHOCOLATE CREME POTS
P{34}

MANGO GINGER COCONUT ICE CREAM
P{35}

COCONUT CHOCOLATE MACAROONS
P{36}

CHOCOLATE CHIA PUDDING
P{37}

Ancestral Chef

And More Dessert Recipes...

PSEUDO
ALMOND
TOFFEE
P{38}

FROZEN
CHOCOLATE
COFFEE
TRUFFLES
P{39}

P{40}

BONUS RECIPE:
BERRY JELLO

BONUS RECIPE:
VANILLA POUND CAKE

P{41}

P{42}

BONUS RECIPE:
CHOCOLATE TRUFFLES

Ancestral Chef

How and Why
TO USE THIS BOOK

Just because you want to be healthy doesn't mean that you should have to go through life without ever eating any dessert.

However, if you're like me, feeling and looking great is important enough that you don't want to put junk in your body any more. Luckily – to adapt an already-overused cliché – I think you can have your Paleo cake and eat it, too. And the desserts in this book are one easy way to do that.

If you like, feel free to jump straight to the recipes and get started, but I wanted to give you a quick summary of why this book is different and what you can expect.

FIRST, THE WORLD HAS CHANGED:
It's long been assumed that if you just ate desserts in moderation, then you'd be fine.

On one hand, I'm just not very good at moderation, but on the other hand, it really makes no sense. Why put even a small amount of poison in your body? That's not something I want to do.

Fortunately, it's a complete myth that moderation is a good way to go, and it's not true at all that desserts have to be made from toxic junk in order to be delicious. This is one of the things that being Paleo has taught me.

I CAN STILL MAKE DELICIOUS FOOD WITHOUT HARMFUL TOXINS, AND YOU CAN TOO:
Also, mainstream nutrition and the media asserted for a very long time that chemically-manufactured, low-fat foods were the healthy way to go.

Nothing could be further from the truth, and you probably already know this. That's why all of my recipes focus on ingredients that are full of natural and healthy fats, proteins, vitamins, and minerals.

In other words, we're no longer living in a world filled with myths about what's healthy and what's not. We know now that real food and real ingredients have kept us, our grandparents, and our ancestors healthy for a very long time.

ALL OF THAT BRINGS ME TO THIS....

WHY THE DESSERTS IN THIS BOOK ARE FANTASTIC:
Above all else, there are 3 main reasons why the desserts in this book are different and better than most:

Ancestral Chef

1. My Desserts will Make You Feel Better, Not Worse

I don't personally believe in or eat things like processed sugars, seed oils, gluten, or a variety of other toxins. So none of the recipes in this book contain any of those ingredients.

As a result, my desserts are much less likely to cause digestive issues, to make you fat, or to make you sick. And that's really important to me. I want to take great care of my own body, but I also want to nourish my family and friends.

I use only real, whole foods, all of which are 100% Paleo, such as coconut oil, local raw honey, coconut flour, and other nutritious foods.

2. My Desserts are Fast

This is almost as important to me as being healthy, because I know that if a recipe is really hard and takes a long time, then we probably won't ever use it.

Every single recipe in this book requires less than 30 minutes of preparation time. And all but 5 recipes can be eaten within 30 minutes after you first start preparing them (most of those 5 recipes need a few hours in the fridge or freezer to set prior to eating)! I'm not kidding. It's that important to me.

3. Every Recipe is Tested to be Awesome

I can't tell you how many recipes I've tried from books where it's clear that the author just made some substitutions and never actually tested the recipe. This is particularly true for Paleo recipes, where people will often just guess that a Paleo ingredient will easily substitute for a "standard" one. It almost never works.

I've tested every recipe in this book until I was completely satisfied that it was awesome and delicious. You might like some recipes better than others, but it won't be because one of the recipes didn't work.

Ancestral Chef

PLEASE DON'T MAKE THESE MISTAKES!

My recipes are very simple, very easy, and very good. But there are two mistakes that I see a lot of people make:

1. Not Following the Recipe Exactly

Obviously, I would never discourage experimenting. But when it comes to many of the Paleo ingredients (like coconut flour), a small change can make a big difference. So if you're trying any of these recipes out for the first time, try to follow the recipe as closely as possible. I've tested them a number of different ways, and the methods in this book work. I've listed some possible substitutions in the "Ingredients and Equipment" chapter, but please note that all substitutions will change the recipe in some way.

2. Not Listening to Your Own Body

All of the ingredients in this book are natural, non-toxic, and nutritious. But that's not a 100% guarantee that your body handles every ingredient well. If you make a dessert and then feel bad after eating it, then your body probably doesn't tolerate one of the ingredients well. It might be the fiber in the coconut, it might be the phytates in the almonds, or it might be the casein in eggs. Whatever it is, listen to your body, because that's what really matters in the end.

START WITH THE BUTTER COOKIES OR BANANA BREAD

You can start wherever you like, but the recipes that consistently get the highest praise from my friends and family are the Amazing Butter Cookies and the Microwave Banana Bread. Don't say I didn't warn you, though, because you'll have to make a new batch very soon after the first! :)

QUESTIONS?

Let me know if you have any questions. You can find me on Facebook, Twitter, Instagram, and Google+ all with the handle AncestralChef. Or you can email me at Louise@AncestralChef.com.

WANT MORE RECIPES?

Check out my blog, www.AncestralChef.com, where I put up new recipes all the time!

Introduction -
How to Not HATE Being Paleo

Have you ever wished that it were just a little bit easier to eat Paleo?

Or do you ever really want a food that you used to eat, only to be disappointed when you realize how terrible it would make you feel?

How about when you have friends or family over? Wouldn't it be great if you could quickly and easily prepare dishes that they'd love but that would still be Paleo?

Well, I want all of that.

And I believe it's all possible. *But I didn't always think so.*

Just two days after I decided to try Paleo, I was more than a little bit angry at my husband, Jeremy.

"Are you kidding me? I can't eat this again!" (I'm not at my best when I'm hungry.)

There was nothing in the fridge except a few boiled eggs and some turkey.

Jeremy was completely fine eating boiled eggs and turkey all day long and for several days in a row. I most definitely was not OK with that.

AT THAT MOMENT, I HATED PALEO. I COULDN'T IMAGINE A WORSE DIET.

Ancestral Chef

I was hungry and miserable because there was nothing I could eat. (Of course, there were actually plenty of things that I could have eaten, but nothing that I considered delicious enough.)

"Well, let's cook something then."

This was Jeremy's attempt to placate me, since – as I noted already – I'm pretty sure he had no objection to eating eggs and turkey for dinner again.

Looking back, if I hadn't been so hungry and miserable, I probably would have thought this suggestion of cooking something was hilarious. Surely, he must have been kidding.

I was NOT someone who cooked.

I was someone who really enjoyed eating, but certainly not cooking. Big difference.

After all, why would anyone *ever* cook?

It was so easy to go to the store, buy some delicious frozen food, and then microwave it. Or better yet, why not just order take-out or delivery?

In college, I survived almost completely on instant ramen noodles or the occasional frozen chicken pot pie (when they were on sale). And after moving to New York for law school, deli sandwiches and Thai take-out were daily rituals.

Of course, that wasn't going to work with Paleo. So despite my initial scoff at Jeremy's suggestion of cooking something for dinner…

I DID start cooking.

Very slowly.

It's not even that I was so opposed to doing it. The bigger obstacle was that I was finishing up law school and then I quickly started working long hours at a big law firm in New York City.

Ancestral Chef

Let's just say all of that left me with very *little time or energy* for cooking. Most nights I would come home very tired and very unmotivated to spend time cooking.

I quickly realized that 2 major hurdles stood in my way of being healthy:

1. **Learning** how to cook **delicious food that is healthy, and**

2. **Finding the** time to cook **these amazing foods (since you can't buy many pre-cooked Paleo foods).**

So in order to consistently stay Paleo, I was forced to find ways to become as efficient as possible at cooking great food. Things just had to move faster. And that applied to everything – from appetizers to entrees to desserts.

That's what I've been blogging about and helping people with since the day I started my blog (AncestralChef.com).
And it's been fantastic to be able to help so many other people just by sharing my own experiences, my own recipes, and everything I've learned. Here's just a quick sample of the kind of responses that keep me motivated:

"Some really great ideas I can implement easily since the busiest time of the year is coming fast!" ~Mary

"Thank you for this recipe. This is so amazing – easy and delicious! I made it already three times today – the first time to see how it turns out, the other times because it was so good." ~Myra

Ancestral Chef

And equally as exciting, I've been able to "wow" friends and family when they come over for a Paleo dinner. Everyone always leaves being surprised at how delicious Paleo can be!

One of my fondest recent memories is when my friend Theresa came over to my apartment with Agapi Stassinopoulos (author of Unbinding the Heart and sister to Arianna Huffington). Agapi, whom I immediately fell in love with, tried one of my vanilla Paleo muffins, and she loved them so much that she took several home to have for breakfast the next morning.

I think most people have an experience similar to mine at first. It's easy to hate Paleo when you're starting out, since it seems so restrictive – there seems to be just nothing to eat.

But when anyone tries desserts made with real, nutritious Paleo ingredients, they're totally shocked. And that can be a powerful turning point for almost anybody – the simple act of realizing

that food can still be delicious while also being healthy.

In the end, that's why I decided to write this book. No life should be without desserts, but you deserve to eat delicious desserts that are going to nourish your body and keep you feeling and looking great. And equally as important, you need recipes that are fast and simple, because there are plenty of complicated and time-consuming recipes out there.

And that's what this book is all about – easy and quick but amazingly delicious desserts that will WOW you, your family, and your friends, regardless of your diet.

I hope you enjoy it, and if you do, then please also check out my blog at AncestralChef.com, and please – if you've bought this book from Amazon, leave me a rating and review so that other people can also experience the joy of delicious Paleo desserts!

Ancestral Chef

Ingredients
and
Equipment

Cooking gluten-free, grain-free, Paleo desserts can be daunting at first just because the ingredients are so unfamiliar.

In order to make your life easier (and mine as well), I've stuck to the most common (and most essential) Paleo ingredients. Although these ingredients are "common" to Paleo recipes, they may not be 100% familiar for you.

Here is a brief list and description of these ingredients, as well as some options for substitutions (or how to make your own) if you have trouble finding or buying any particular ingredient.

ALMOND FLOUR:

Almond flour is a flour-like substance made from almonds (usually "blanched," meaning without the skin) that have been ground.

You can make this yourself by grinding almonds in a food processor or blender. However, if you make it yourself, it usually won't result in a very fine flour, which might change the texture of a recipe; also, blending for too long will produce almond butter rather than almond flour.

You can get away with using your own ground almond flour (often called almond meal) in the recipes in this book, but it will make the texture of the desserts a bit grainier.

© picsfive - Fotolia.com

COCONUT FLOUR:

Coconut flour is dehydrated and defatted coconut flakes (or shredded coconut) ground very finely until it forms a flour.

You can make a rough version of coconut flour yourself by grinding unsweetened raw coconut flakes (or shredded coconut) in a blender or food processor. Again, you have to be careful not to over-blend it, as it'll form coconut butter instead. To get a fine flour requires a bit more work – you'd need to first blend the coconut flakes (or shredded coconut) with water, strain the liquid out, and then dry the resulting meal in a dehydrator or oven.

I highly recommend buying coconut flour if you can, since many of the recipes work much better with fine coconut flour.

COCONUT OIL:

Coconut oil is simply the oil from coconuts – I do NOT recommend trying to make it yourself. Just buy it (it's also great to use as your general cooking oil).

If you can't find any coconut oil to buy, then try using another healthy Paleo oil like ghee (see below) or olive oil (this will change the taste, of course!). If you are not sensitive to dairy, then butter (preferably grass-fed) is also an option, although if you have access to butter, then I highly suggest making your own ghee using the butter.

GHEE:

Ghee is basically the oil derived from removing all milk solids from butter (this makes it healthier than butter because many people have sensitivities to those milk solids). It's also referred to as clarified butter, although ghee is typically made in a slightly different process than clarified butter. You can buy ghee or clarified butter in many stores. It's particularly popular in South Asian cuisines as well as certain European cuisines, like traditional French cooking.

You can make your own ghee by gently heating unsalted butter until the milk solids (the white residue) separate from the oil. Strain the liquid through cheesecloth to remove all of the solids, and the oil you're left with is the ghee/clarified butter. Typically ghee involves a bit more effort, but for the recipes in this book, the resulting oil is fine to use as ghee.

RAW HONEY:

One of the biggest problems with Paleo desserts is finding a good Paleo sweetener.

No matter what you use, this is probably the least healthy part of any Paleo dessert. I personally believe that raw honey is the best (and tastiest) Paleo sweetener, since it contains many of the vitamins and minerals needed for your body to properly process the sugar in the honey. (I don't, though, believe that honey is great for our bodies in huge amounts, so I try to use it judiciously.)

If you don't have access to raw honey, then most natural sugars (e.g. regular honey, pure maple syrup, and cane sugar) are about equivalent from a health perspective, so pick whichever is more convenient for you. You will have to adjust the amounts if you're using a sweetener other than honey as they differ in sweetness.

STEVIA:

This is a natural sugar substitute that adds very few carbs or calories but is several hundred times the sweetness of sugar. It has a slightly bitter aftertaste, which is why I don't like to use it by itself in desserts (unless I'm making a sugar-free one for my dad, who is diabetic). However, honey and spices hide the taste of stevia well so that you can decrease the amount of honey and substitute in some stevia to create a low-sugar dessert.

While some people place stevia into the same category as artificial sweeteners, it's certainly healthier than copious amounts of honey and maple syrup, and the amounts of stevia that need to be used are tiny.

There is a variety of different brands of stevia (some are more pure than others, and some have other sugars or fillers mixed in). I prefer to buy very pure stevia and just add a tiny amount into my baked goods. You are welcome to use whatever brand you like (or not use stevia at all), but I encourage you to use a stevia that doesn't have other fillers or sugars added in. If you use a non-pure brand of stevia, then be sure to use that brand's conversion chart.

© dream79 - Fotolia.com

Ancestral Chef

30-Minute Paleo Dessert Recipes | 15

If you don't want to use stevia for whatever reason, then simply use raw honey (or your sweetener of choice) instead.

VANILLA EXTRACT:

I love adding pure vanilla extract to various desserts – it imparts a taste of sweetness without having any sugar in it. Some store-bought vanilla extracts contain added sugar, so try to buy ones that don't list any forms of sugar in the ingredients. You can also make your own vanilla extract by using fresh vanilla beans (split them in half) and letting them sit in some flavorless alcohol (e.g. vodka) for 2-3 months.

If you don't have access to vanilla extract or vanilla beans, you can omit this ingredient from the recipes (this will change the flavor of the recipes a bit).

COCONUT CREAM:

Coconut cream is really just a thicker version of coconut milk (it's great as a non-dairy substitute for cream). The easiest way to get this is to buy cans of coconut milk (it's best to buy ones where the ingredients are just coconut and water) and to place the cans in the refrigerated for half a day. The coconut cream will form on the top of the can so that you can scoop it out from the top when you open the can gently.

To make your own coconut cream, you can food process fresh coconut meat (scraped from fresh coconuts) until it forms a creamy puree.

COCONUT BUTTER:

Coconut butter is dried unsweetened coconut flakes (or shredded coconut) pureed until the oils mix with the coconut meat (note that there isn't water in this).

You can buy coconut butter in jars from many gourmet or natural health stores, but you can also make this yourself using unsweetened coconut flakes (or shredded coconut) and blending or food processing it really well (you may need to add a little bit of coconut oil to help it blend).

CHIA SEEDS:

Chia seeds are small plant seeds that have gelatinous properties, which makes them great for grain-free baking (it helps bind ingredients together). Chia seeds are sold all over the world and have become increasingly popular in the US over the past few years.

If you can't find chia seeds, then you can use flax seeds instead (chia is generally considered healthier than flax). If you don't have access to either, then you can add in an extra egg (note that this will change the texture and taste of the recipe). However, these substitutions won't work for the Chocolate Chia Pudding Recipe because chia is the main ingredient.

BAKING SODA AND BAKING POWDER:

Baking powder is usually a combination of baking soda with an acidic agent (such as cream of tartar, which is described below) along with some other ingredients, such as cornstarch. Baking powder produces carbon dioxide bubbles, which expand in the oven (due to the heat) so that your baked goods will rise and become light and soft.

Baking soda is 100% sodium bicarbonate, which reacts with anything acidic in your baking mixture to produce carbon dioxide bubbles. These bubbles will start forming as soon as the baking soda touches the acidic ingredients.

While you can't make your own baking soda (since it's just the pure compound of sodium bicarbonate), you can make your own baking powder from baking soda and cream of tartar (which is a naturally

occurring acidic salt, potassium hydrogen tartrate).

1 teaspoon baking powder = 1/4 teaspoon baking soda + 1/2 teaspoon cream of tartar

One advantage of making your own baking powder is that your baking won't include cornstarch or any other non-caking agent that is typically put into store-bought baking powder to prevent it from clumping together.

© Brent Hofacker - Fotolia.com

Ancestral Chef

EQUIPMENT REQUIRED FOR THE RECIPES IN THIS BOOK:

- Oven
- Microwave (I know some people object to microwaves, but they are a super convenient, very safe, and very fast way of cooking!)
- Muffin or cupcake pan (with cupcake liners so you don't have to wash as many dishes)
- Mixing bowl
- Electric whisk or mixer (generally only needed for whipping egg whites, which you can technically do by hand)
- Blender or food processor

Essential
Baking Conversions for Non-US Readers

Growing up in England, I remember first hearing about US cup measurements in recipes and wondering which cup from my cupboard I was supposed to use to measure out the amount. It seemed like a crazy system to me! So, I'm sure for those of you who are unused to the US measurement system, my recipes may look like gobbledygook.

That's why I've included these handy conversion charts to help you out.

All oven temperatures have already been converted to Celsius in each recipe for you.

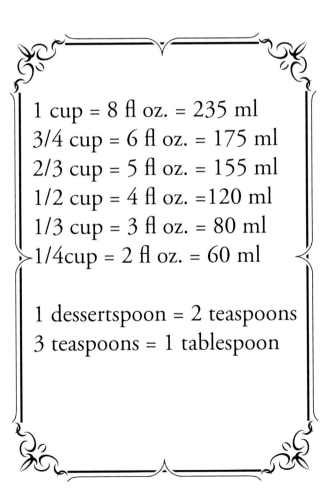

1 cup = 8 fl oz. = 235 ml
3/4 cup = 6 fl oz. = 175 ml
2/3 cup = 5 fl oz. = 155 ml
1/2 cup = 4 fl oz. =120 ml
1/3 cup = 3 fl oz. = 80 ml
1/4cup = 2 fl oz. = 60 ml

1 dessertspoon = 2 teaspoons
3 teaspoons = 1 tablespoon

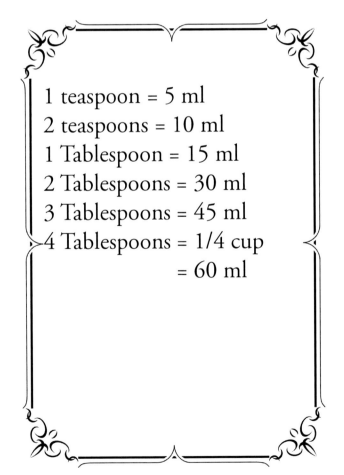

1 teaspoon = 5 ml
2 teaspoons = 10 ml
1 Tablespoon = 15 ml
2 Tablespoons = 30 ml
3 Tablespoons = 45 ml
4 Tablespoons = 1/4 cup
= 60 ml

Ancestral Chef

Chocolate Brownies

Getting these to be perfectly moist and yet flavorful was not easy, especially since I wanted to reduce the sugar in them and add in some stevia (you can, of course, put in more honey instead of the stevia). It took me a while to perfect these brownies, but it was worth it (Jeremy loves chocolate brownies)!

INGREDIENTS

- 3/4 cup almond flour
- 1/4 cup coconut flour
- 4 eggs
- 2/3 cup coconut oil
- 4 Tablespoons raw honey
- Stevia equivalent to 3 Tablespoons of sugar
- 2/3 cup cocoa powder
- 1/8 teaspoon salt
- 1/2 teaspoon vanilla extract
- 1/2 Tablespoons apple cider vinegar (optional – helps the brownies rise)
- 1 teaspoon baking soda

DIRECTIONS

1. Preheat oven to 350F (175C).
2. Mix all the ingredients together well (add in the baking soda last).
3. Pour into 12 muffin cups.
4. Bake at 350F for 17 minutes.

No-Bake Apple Pies

Makes 2 small ramekins (but can be scaled pretty easily without much extra effort or cooking time).

My obsession with apple pies led me to make a full-fledged Paleo apple pie complete with Paleo pastry and lattice. That has been the most popular recipe on my blog, but it was so time-consuming that I couldn't make it all the time, and so this no-bake apple pie recipe was born.

INGREDIENTS

- 2 apples, peeled and chopped into small pieces
- 1/2 Tablespoon vanilla extract
- 1 cup unsalted chopped nuts (almonds, pecans, macadamia nuts) – you can use a blender or food processor to roughly chop these
- 2 Tablespoons coconut oil
- 2 Tablespoons ghee (or replace with another 2 Tablespoons coconut oil)
- 6 whole raw almonds as topping
- 1/2 teaspoon cinnamon
- Pinch of ground nutmeg
- Pinch of ground cloves

DIRECTIONS

1. Melt 2 tablespoons of coconut oil and 2 tablespoons of ghee in a saucepan on medium heat.
2. Add the apples to the saucepan and stir regularly to cook the apples until they're soft (8-10 minutes).
3. Add in the vanilla extract, cinnamon, nutmeg, cloves, and the chopped nuts and cook for 5 more minutes so that the flavor sinks in.
4. Divide into 2 individual ramekins, packing it down and making sure that you don't scoop out the extra oil at the bottom of the pan.
5. Place the 6 whole raw almonds into the extra oil left in the pan to coat them (it gives them a glistening look and some flavor).
6. Place 3 almonds (in a clover leaf arrangement) on top of each apple pie as a decoration.

Ancestral Chef

Amazing Butter Cookies

Makes approx. 8 medium-sized cookies

Have you ever had amazing shortbread cookies that just burst with butter flavor? Well, meet the Paleo version! For most recipes in this book, you can use coconut oil instead of ghee, but please note that such a substitution would significantly change the flavor of this recipe.

INGREDIENTS

- 1 1/2 cups almond flour
- 1/2 cup coconut flour
- 2 eggs
- 1/2 cup ghee
- 2 teaspoon vanilla extract
- 4 Tablespoons raw honey

DIRECTIONS

1. Preheat oven to 325F (160C).
2. Combine all the ingredients in a mixing bowl.
3. Form palm-sized cookies (2-inch diameter) with the dough and place on a parchment paper-lined baking tray.
4. Bake at 325F for 12 minutes.
5. Cool for 5 minutes before removing from parchment paper.

Microwave Banana Bread

Makes 1 banana bread (approx. 1 cup)

This is the fastest recipe in this book! It's moist and sweet without any sugar (except from the banana). I love this recipe because I can make it in the office or anywhere with a microwave!

INGREDIENTS

- 1/3 cup almond flour
- 1 Tablespoon coconut oil, melted
- 1/2 ripe banana
- 1/2 teaspoon baking powder
- 1/8 teaspoon salt
- 1/2 teaspoon vanilla extract (optional)

DIRECTIONS

1. Mix all the ingredients together in a microwaveable mug – mash the banana in with a fork.
2. Microwave on high for 90 to 120 seconds (1.5 to 2 minutes).
3. Let cool for 5 minutes and eat from the mug or gently tip out onto a plate.

Ancestral Chef

Chocolate Coconut Fudge Cups

Makes 6 chocolate fudge cups

The hardest part of making this recipe is waiting for it to freeze! It's got a great fudge consistency and is fantastic for chocolate lovers.

INGREDIENTS

- 1 cup cocoa powder
- 1/4 cup honey
- 1/2 cup coconut cream (from the top of a refrigerated can of coconut milk)
- 1/4 cup coconut butter

DIRECTIONS

1. Place the coconut butter, coconut cream, and honey in a bowl and melt just slightly in the microwave or over a bowl of hot water. You want the mixture to be almost runny so that it's easy to mix everything together.
2. Add the cocoa powder into the bowl and mix well.
3. Spoon the mixture into 6 muffin cups.
4. Freeze for 15 minutes.
5. Store leftovers in the fridge.

Ancestral Chef

Mini Pumpkin Pie

Makes 1 small ramekin

Despite being a huge pie fan growing up (probably something to do with the fact I grew up in England), I actually never had a pumpkin pie until I came to America and went to a Thanksgiving dinner. I loved the idea and taste of using a vegetable in a sweet dessert dish.

However, I didn't love how time-consuming making a pumpkin pie from scratch was, so here's a super fast version.

INGREDIENTS

- 6 Tablespoons pumpkin puree (from a can or else boiled pumpkin pieces pureed)
- 3 Tablespoons ghee
- 3 Tablespoons pure cocoa powder
- 1/2 teaspoon pumpkin pie spice (ground cinnamon, ginger, nutmeg, cloves)
- Sweetener of choice (optional – I sometimes eat it unsweetened)

DIRECTIONS

1. Place all ingredients into a microwaveable bowl and microwave on high for approx. 45 seconds (just to soften everything and make it easier to blend).
2. Blend well in blender or mixer.
3. Serve warm, or chill in refrigerator for a more solid consistency.

Ancestral Chef

Pineapple Mango Banana Sorbet

Makes 2 small ramekins

I've tried to make Paleo ice creams and sorbets on many occasions, but they always end u
as an icy chunk because I don't have an ice maker. However, this "sorbet" is amazing and
ready to serve immediately without the use of an ice maker! The banana gives it a really
creamy texture – I love it!

INGREDIENTS

- 1/2 cup frozen pineapples
- 1 cup frozen mango pieces
- 1 banana, room temperature
- Stevia equivalent to 4 Tablespoons of sugar (optional)
- 1/2 Tablespoon fresh lime juice
- 1 banana for topping

DIRECTIONS

1. Blend really really well in a blender. Depending on how good your blender is, you may have to blend briefly and then push the frozen fruit down and repeat several times.
2. Top with a few banana slices.
3. Serve immediately.

NOTE: This sorbet goes really well with warm Coconut Banana Balls (page 29).

Coconut Butter Dates

Makes 10 coconut butter dates

I love 2-ingredient recipes – it makes the dessert special (i.e. it's not just a piece of fruit), but at the same time, it's super easy and quick to make.

That's the fantastic thing about this recipe – it looks like you put in effort to make dessert, but it actually took all of 5 minutes!

INGREDIENTS

- 10 pitted dates
- 1 cup coconut butter

DIRECTIONS

1. Melt the coconut butter slightly in the microwave if it's not soft enough to scoop out with a spoon (make sure to take the metal lid off the jar first before microwaving).
2. Slice open each date so that it opens out but isn't sliced in half.
3. Stuff each date with as much coconut butter as you can fit in while still being able to close it up.

2-Ingredient Pancakes

This is another amazing 2-ingredient recipe, and it's delicious – the banana adds all the sweetness so no need for additional sweeteners. This is probably more like a crepe than a traditional American pancake (i.e. it's pretty thin). However, just note that it's easy to burn the batter so take it slowly – one option is to make several smaller pancakes with the batter so that they cook a bit faster.

INGREDIENTS

- 1 banana, peeled
- 1 egg

DIRECTIONS

1. Blend the egg and the banana in a blender to form a batter.
2. Place 1 tablespoon of coconut oil into a frying pan and pour in the batter in a spiral to create a thin pancake.
3. Let the pancake cook for around 10 minutes before flipping it.
4. After flipping it, let the other side cook for around 10 minutes.

Ancestral Chef

Coconut Banana Balls

Makes 12 coconut banana balls

These were so amazing it was shocking! I like them both warm and cold, but if you serve them warm, then serve it with the Pineapple Mango Banana Sorbet for an amazing experience.

INGREDIENTS

- 1 banana
- 2 cups unsweetened shredded coconut
- 1 Tablespoon raw honey
- 2 Tablespoons coconut oil, melted
- 1 teaspoon vanilla extract
- Dash of salt
- Chocolate powder to sprinkle on top (optional)

DIRECTIONS

1. Preheat oven to 250F (120C) if serving warm.
2. Mix all the ingredients together in a bowl.
3. Form small balls (1-inch diameter) from the dough using your hands.
4. Refrigerate or bake at 250F for 15 min.

Sugar-Free Ginger Spice Cookies

Makes approx. 12 medium-sized cookies

My dad is diabetic, so I'm always trying to find ways to make tasty treats for him that won't raise his blood sugar levels. This is one of them! A great way to add a bit of extra sweetness for your non-diabetic family and friends is to put in some raisins (or change th stevia to honey).

INGREDIENTS

- 2 cups whole almonds
- 2 Tablespoons chia seeds
- 1/4 cup coconut oil
- 1 egg
- 3 Tablespoons freshly grated ginger
- 2 Tablespoons cinnamon powder
- ½ teaspoon of nutmeg
- Stevia equivalent to 6 Tablespoons of sugar
- Dash of salt

DIRECTIONS

1. Preheat oven to 350F (175C).
2. Food process or blend the whole almonds with the chia seeds.
3. Mix all the ingredients together in a large bowl.
4. Form small cookies with your hands and place on a baking tray lined with parchment paper.
5. Bake at 350F for 15 minutes.

Ancestral Chef

Vanilla Madeleine Cookies

Makes 12 small cookies

These amazing vanilla Madeleine cookies were a complete mistake. I was trying to make Paleo French Macarons, and these popped out! All I can say is that they taste remarkably like Madeleines, which are delicious!

INGREDIENTS

- 2/3 cup almond flour
- 4 Tablespoons raw honey
- 3 large egg whites
- Stevia equivalent to 3 Tablespoons of sugar
- 1 and 1/2 teaspoons vanilla extract

DIRECTIONS

1. Preheat oven to 350F (175C).
2. Beat the egg whites using an electric mixer until peaks form.
3. Fold in the almond flour, honey, stevia, and vanilla extract.
4. Using a spoon, drop small dollops of the mixture onto a baking tray lined with parchment paper.
5. Bake for 12 minutes until slightly golden on top (they burn quickly so remove immediately).
6. Let cool before peeling off the parchment paper.

Raw Coconut Cookies

These miniature cookies are a bit tricky if you don't get the ingredient proportions just right (because you're relying on the coconut oil and the honey to hold everything together). But apart from that, these are super easy and delicious!

INGREDIENTS

- 2 Tablespoons coconut oil, melted
- 2 Tablespoons raw honey
- 1/2 cup unsweetened shredded coconut
- 1/2 cup ground almonds
- Chocolate chips for topping (optional)

DIRECTIONS

1. Mix all the ingredients together well.
2. Using your hands, form small cookies and place on a plate to refrigerate (placing a piece of parchment paper on the plate helps).
3. Refrigerate for 15 minutes.

Ancestral Chef

Sugar-Free Chocolate Biscotti

Makes 8 pieces

This is another recipe that my dad especially enjoys. It's lightly sweetened with stevia and has a great flavor to it with the cocoa powder and coconut. When it first comes out of the oven, it's pretty soft still, but you can let it dry out for longer by leaving it in the oven at a very low temperature or just by sitting it out. Or don't bother waiting and just enjoy immediately.

INGREDIENTS

- 2 cups whole almonds
- 2 Tablespoons chia seeds
- 1/4 cup unsweetened shredded coconut
- 1 egg
- 1/4 cup coconut oil
- 1/4 cocoa powder
- Stevia equivalent to 2-3 Tablespoons of sugar
- 1/4 teaspoon salt
- 1 teaspoon baking soda

DIRECTIONS

1. Preheat oven to 350F (175C).
2. Food process or blend the whole almonds with the chia seeds (the mixture should be fairly fine).
3. Mix all the ingredients together well.
4. Place the dough on a piece of aluminum foil to shape into 8 biscotti-shaped slices (long thin fingers). (Or you could refrigerate the dough for 30 minutes in a loaf shape and then carefully slice it.)
5. Bake at 350F for 12 minutes.
6. Enjoy warm (it'll be soft), or let it dry further in the oven at a low temperature, or else leave out overnight.

Ancestral Chef

Coffee Chocolate Pot de Crème

It always seems so sexy (or perhaps just European) to finish a meal off with some coffee. So, these coffee-flavored coconut pots de crème seemed perfect.

INGREDIENTS

- 1/4 cup cocoa powder
- 2 teaspoons ground coffee beans
- 2 Tablespoons raw honey
- 6 Tablespoons coconut cream
- 1 teaspoon vanilla extract

DIRECTIONS

1. Blend everything well.
2. Pour mixture into small espresso cups.
3. Refrigerate for 20 minutes before serving.

Mango Ginger Coconut Ice Cream

Makes 2 small ramekins

I gave up dairy ice-cream a while ago, so it's wonderful to be able to enjoy creamy Paleo "ice cream" still.

INGREDIENTS

- 1 cup frozen mango chunks
- 1/4 cup coconut cream
- 1/4 cup unsweetened shredded coconut
- 1/2 Tablespoon lime juice
- 1 teaspoon ginger, grated as topping
- 2 Tablespoons raw honey

DIRECTIONS

1. Let the mango chunks defrost for 5 minutes at room temperature.
2. Blend the mango, coconut cream, shredded coconut, lime juice, and raw honey well.
3. Top with the grated ginger.

Coconut Chocolate Macaroons

Makes 24-28 macaroons

These are just the perfect mix of chocolate, sweetness, and toasted coconut. It's soft but with a slight crunch.

INGREDIENTS

- 3 cups unsweetened shredded coconut
- 4 large egg whites
- 2 Tablespoons raw honey
- Tiny dash of pure stevia (approx. 2 Tablespoons worth of sugar)
- 1/4 cup of 100% pure cocoa powder
- 1 teaspoon vanilla extract
- Dash of salt

DIRECTIONS

1. Preheat oven to 350F (175C).
2. Beat the egg whites with an electric whisk until peaks form.
3. Add in the raw honey, stevia, cocoa powder, vanilla extract, and salt, and mix well.
4. Lastly, mix in the shredded coconut using a spoon.
5. Bake for 15 minutes.

Ancestral Chef

Chocolate Chia Pudding

Chia seeds are fantastic for making pudding (the seeds puff up when soaked so you get a tapioca-like dessert).

INGREDIENTS

- 2 Tablespoons unsweetened cocoa powder
- 1 cup unsweetened coconut milk
- 1/3 cup chia seeds
- 1 Tablespoon unsweetened shredded coconut (for topping)
- Spices and/or sweetener of choice (I didn't use any spices or sweeteners as there was a tad bit of sweetness from the coconut milk naturally)

DIRECTIONS

1. Mix together all the ingredients in a bowl.
2. Cover the bowl and refrigerate overnight (approx. 6-10 hours).
3. Blend the mixture until smooth (this helped to get all the cocoa powder nicely mixed in).

Pseudo Almond Toffee

Makes approx. 8 2-by-2-inch squares

Toffee is traditionally made from butter and sugar, both very non-paleo ingredients. However, I was determined to experiment to see if I could get something toffee-like, and did with ghee and raw honey.

Note that you should refrigerate for a few hours to get a toffee-like consistency (the ghee will separate from the honey to form 2-layers, but it'll taste like toffee together).

INGREDIENTS

- 1/4 cup honey
- 2 T ghee
- 1/2 cup whole almonds
- 1/2 teaspoon salt

DIRECTIONS

1. Combine the honey and ghee in a pot over medium heat while stirring.
2. Keep stirring until they start combining (they'll never fully combine).
3. Add in the almonds and the salt.
4. Pour onto a piece of parchment page and place in refrigerator to cool.

Frozen Chocolate Coffee Truffles

Makes approx. 6 truffles

I had an epiphany one night in bed - why not use the ice-cube tray to make frozen coconut butter desserts!

It took me a few weeks before finally getting around to trying it out, but the recipe was an instant success - it tasted great despite the super low honey amount!

Note that while this is another really easy recipe, it does require a bit of time sitting in the freezer. I love making a large batch of these to sit in the freezer for whenever.

INGREDIENTS

- 1/2 cup coconut butter
- 3 Tablespoons 100% cocoa powder
- 1 Tablespoon ground coffee
- 1 Tablespoon unsweetened shredded coconut
- 1/2 teaspoon raw honey
- 1 Tablespoon coconut oil

DIRECTIONS

1. Melt the coconut butter (in a microwave) so that it can be mixed easily with a fork.
2. Mix in all the ingredients (except the coconut oil) and mix well with a fork.
3. Take an ice cube tray and pour approximately 1/4 teaspoon of coconut oil into 6-7 of the cups.
4. Spoon the mixture into each cup of the ice cube tray and gently pat them flat with a fork.
5. Freeze for 4-5 hours.
6. Defrost at room temperature for 15-20 minutes before serving.

Ancestral Chef

BONUS RECIPE: Chocolate Truffles

Makes approx. 10 truffles

I had never given much thought to what chocolate truffles were made of before going Paleo, but then I started noticing that most store-bought truffles contain all sorts of ingredients that I stay away from (e.g., vegetable oil, soy lecithin, corn syrup). And that's why I decided to make my own using coconut oil.

This recipe uses 85% dark chocolate, but you can use 100% chocolate and add in raw honey instead.

INGREDIENTS

- 3.5oz 85% dark chocolate
- 1 tablespoon coconut oil
- 1/4 cup coconut cream (skim from the top of a refrigerated can of coconut milk)
- 1 tablespoon brandy or other alcohol or 1 tablespoon vanilla extract
- Coatings: 100% chocolate powder, unsweetened shredded coconut, or chopped nuts

DIRECTIONS

1. Place the chocolate in a microwave-proof bowl and melt using 30 second cycles.
2. Melt the coconut oil in the microwave separately and add to the melted chocolate. Stir together.
3. While the mixture is still warm, quickly add in the coconut milk (try to use milk that's at room temperature) and the alcohol or vanilla extract. Mix well.
4. Place in freezer for 2 hours.
5. After removing from the freezer, let it thaw for 5-10 minutes so that the chocolate is soft enough to scoop out with a spoon.
6. Using a melon scoop or just using a spoon, scoop out small chunks of chocolate and form it into balls in your hands.
7. Add the coating of your choice by rolling the chocolate ball through the coating.

Ancestral Chef

BONUS RECIPE:
Berry Jello

Makes 2 cups

I love this simple berry Jello (we call it jelly in England) made without any added sugar (the only sugar is from the fresh fruit puree). It has a slightly different consistency to traditional Jello (this is more mousse-like) because of fiber from the berries. To make more traditional Jello, just remove the fiber by passing the puree through a cheese cloth (or using a juicer if you have one).

INGREDIENTS

- 1 cup of strawberries
- 1 cup of blueberries
- 2 tablespoons of gelatin powder
- 1 cup of water

DIRECTIONS

1. Puree the strawberries and blueberries.
2. Pour the pureed fruit into cups, filling each cup half way.
3. Place 2 tablespoons of the gelatin powder into a large bowl and add in 1 cup of cold water. Stir well. Then place the bowl into the microwave and heat on high for 1 minute. Mix well using a fork.
4. Pour the gelatin water into the cups with the fruit puree (almost filling each cup to the brim) and mix well.
5. Leave in the fridge to set for 3-4 hours.
6. Serve with a few slices of strawberries as garnish.

BONUS RECIPE:
Vanilla Pound Cake

Makes 1 loaf

This pound cake never ceases to WOW. It's just so much like real pound cake.

The secret ingredient is a tiny amount of whey protein powder, which is just one of the proteins purified from milk. Most concerns with whey protein powder stem from the fact that many brands are packed with artificial sweeteners, colors, and flavors, so I suggest buying a pure one.

INGREDIENTS

- 3 cups almond flour
- 1/3 cup pure whey protein powder
- 1 and 1/2 teaspoons baking powder
- 1 teaspoon baking soda
- Pinch of salt
- 1/2 cup of ghee, softened
- 3 large eggs
- 1 tablespoon vanilla extract (sugar-free)
- 4 Tablespoons honey
- Stevia equivalent to 1/2 cup sugar
- 1/2 cup almond milk

DIRECTIONS

1. Preheat oven to 300F (150C).
2. Butter a loaf pan (9in-by-5in).
3. Mix all the ingredients together well.
4. Pour the batter into the loaf pan and bake for 60 minutes (the cake will rise in the oven and the top should turn golden brown). Let the cake cool for a few minutes before flipping it out. Cut into slices when it's completely cooled.

Ancestral Chef

17329115R00025

Made in the USA
Middletown, DE
18 January 2015